CHARLTON

CHARLTON

PICTURING CHANGE

WILLIAM O. HULTGREN & QUENTIN R. KUEHL

Charleston · London

THE
History
PRESS

Published by The History Press
Charleston, SC 29403
www.historypress.net

Cover design by Natasha Momberger

First published 2008

Manufactured in the United States

ISBN 978.1.59629.564.3

Library of Congress Cataloging-in-Publication Data

Hultgren, William O.
Charlton : picturing change / William O. Hultgren and Quentin R. Kuehl.
p. cm.
ISBN 978-1-59629-564-3
1. Charlton (Mass. : Town)--History--Pictorial works. 2. Charlton (Mass. : Town)--Rural conditions--Pictorial
works. 3. Social change--Massachusetts--Charlton (Town)--History--Pictorial works. I. Kuehl, Quentin R. II.
Title.
F74.C42H85 2008
974.4'3--dc22
                                            2008031395

CONTENTS

CHARLTON

A Century in Pictures

How do you tell the tale of a century? One of the best ways is through pictures. Thus, this book represents a collection of treasured photographs that tell a story of the town of Charlton from the turn of the century in 1900 to the beginning of the millennium in the year 2000. Eclectic in nature, these pictures represent a wide variety of glimpses into the everyday lives of the citizens of Charlton across the decades, as well as a record of many significant people, places and events that are a part of the town's rich history. For Charlton, the twentieth century marked a major transformation, as the town evolved from a small rural community of farms, open spaces, fields, pastures, rolling hills, lakes and woods into a sprawling, steadily growing residential community.

With an area of 43.8 square miles, Charlton, established in 1755, has always been considered large in size—it is the third largest in Worcester County—yet in terms of population, records show that there were only 2,075 citizens here in Charlton at the turn of the century. At that time, it has been said that Charlton could boast having more cows than people! However, by the end of the century, demographics had changed significantly. The year 2000 census reported 11,263 citizens. Not only had the horse 'n buggies and dirt roads disappeared, but there were also no working dairy farms left within the town. Thus, for Charlton, this span of one hundred years was one of tremendous change.

At first, this transformation was gradual, but it became more pronounced in the last decade of the century. Many changes in the late 1980s and the 1990s were sparked, in the opinion of many longtime Charlton residents, by an article that appeared in the *Boston Globe* in the mid-1980s that spoke of the tranquil beauty of Charlton's rural setting, the abundance of buildable land, its good schools, relatively low taxes and its proximity to major highways and cities. Up until the publication of this newspaper piece, Charlton had been one of the state's best-kept secrets! However, as the profitability of farming declined and young people sought professions in other sectors of our nation's changing economy, farms were sold. Acreage was divided into house lots and subdivisions with many new roads and streets that would give today's visitor to Charlton a completely different impression of the town than would have been the case in 1900, 1950 or even in 1975, when the town celebrated its 220th birthday.

Originally, Charlton was composed of numerous villages in different sections of the town, such as the Center, marked by the town common, Dexter Memorial Hall and Charlton High School; the Depot, where it once was possible to board the train for Worcester or Springfield; and the City, where the woolen mills operated for so many years.

In these early days, Charlton's many villages were served by several district schoolhouses. These one-room schools were eventually replaced by Charlton's common elementary and secondary schools, but by the close of the century, they had evolved into a regional system to serve the public school students of Charlton.

Unquestionably, the twentieth century brought significant change to our world, our nation, our state and our local community. Charlton represents a microcosm of these enormous changes to our way of life. Yet, through it all, Charlton has strived to maintain its original character and strong sense of community. Thus, chronicled within the pages of this book is the story of a beautiful small town, loved by all who live here, but cherished especially by those who were born and raised here and who have lived here for decades. The pictures assembled here reflect the core values of the town's citizens—values and traditions that have sustained them through good times (as in the post–World War II era, with its simplicity of life and its tranquility) and through adversity (as in the Hurricane of 1938 and the tragic flood of 1955). Now, in the twenty-first century, Charlton stands ready to move forward, well rooted in a rich past, but prepared to make additional changes necessary for our new world, confident that it will always remain the kind of community we are all proud to call home.

Linda E. (Stone) Denault, PhD

ACKNOWLEDGEMENTS

The authors wish to thank the following individuals and organizations for the use of illustrations that capture the rich history and the vast changes in the town of Charlton in the twentieth century: Kathy Ham, Cathleen Kuehl, Kenneth Maynard, Francis Lamprey, Gail Phillips, Thelma Jolin, Alfred Arnold, Harold Allard, Horace Pontin, Harvey and Pauline Boudreau, Charlton Historical Society, Daniel Tucker Collection, Melvin Baker Collection, Eva Eastman, Eugene Ide, Philip Becker, Stanley Mann, R. Reed Grimwade, Mildred Mahan, the Robert Ewing Collection, Carl Phillips, Francis Bailey, Jesse Westlund, Carol Pike, John Taylor, Leslie Olney, Ralph Truesdell Estates, Wayne Lund, Kathy Cherinski, Donald Beal, Mary Jane and Tony Gillespie, Alvin Lotti, Wilfred Savoie, Fred Maas and others unknown.

We also wish to thank Marilyn Hultgren, Linnea Sciarappa, Judith Mascall, Linda E. (Stone) Denault and Carol Hill for their work, assistance and encouragement in the publication of this book.

CHARLTON

The town of Charlton was divided early on into thirteen districts for school and highway purposes. These various districts each adopted a name, and several developed into villages. During the twentieth century, Charlton Center (District 1), Dodge (Districts 2, 3, 4), Charlton City (District 13), South Charlton (Districts 5, 6, 7, 8, 9, 10) and Charlton Depot (Districts 11,12) became postal villages. This book groups illustrations into these five geographical areas, as indicated on this map of the township of Charlton, for the benefit of the reader who is not familiar with the town.

CHARLTON
CENTER VILLAGE

One might ask: how did Charlton get its name? The answer is not so simple since it requires a bit of investigation into family connections and eighteenth-century English titles. The portrait of Sir Francis Charlton and its caption, pictured later in this chapter, will help answer this question.

French refugees settled the township of Oxford in the late 1700s. The western part of Oxford was granted to five speculators, who received 1,700-acre portions. In 1731, these lands were offered to individuals in 100-acre "farms." Ebenezer Macintire (McIntire) purchased one of these lots and erected a house in what is today's Charlton Center Village. In one room of his house, he operated a tavern. The men from this western part of Oxford gathered in McIntire's tavern to discuss the proposition that they become a town of their own, as they were six miles from the Oxford meetinghouse and received no benefits for the taxes they paid to Oxford. Three times they petitioned the General Court, and on the third try they were successful. The District of Charlton was founded on January 5, 1755. McIntire gratefully gave the district an acre of land near his tavern for a meetinghouse and training field, or common, thus establishing his property as the Center Village and his tavern patronage from those attending church and musters. A gore of land bordering Charlton on the north, which belonged to no town and was too small to be a township of its own, was annexed to Charlton in 1757, establishing Charlton's boundary as much the same as it is today.

By 1900, the Center Village contained houses strung out on each side of the common, two churches, a store, two schools, two taverns, the animal pound, two cemeteries, a blacksmith, a post office, the telephone exchange and several tradesmen. Charlton Center remained the same until the arrival of the electric street railway or trolley in 1903. Transportation was now available on the electric cars to visit, shop and work outside the village. A luxurious resort hotel was built on the high hill just west of the Center by the Worcester and Southbridge Street Railway in 1903. After only eighteen months, the hotel closed and remained vacant until the Grand Lodge of Masons purchased it for a retirement home for Masons and their spouses. By 1927, the automobile made the trolley obsolete, and the rails were taken up. In 1928, the building of the town's major road, Route 20, bypassed Charlton Center, leaving it outside the business sphere of the town.

A town hall was built in the Center in 1905, the same year a high school was established in the vacated old town hall. The Center was chosen, after a hotly contested town meeting, as the site of a new high school in 1922. The rural, one-room schoolhouses were closed in 1949, and the students were bussed to the expanded high school building, consolidating public education at Charlton Center. When a new elementary school was built, it was located in the Center.

Sir Francis Charlton, baronet (1707–1784), for whom the town of Charlton was named. He was born in the town of Ludford, in Shropshire, England, as the son of Sir Blundel Charlton. He succeeded his father as the fourth baronet in 1742, and was treasurer of the General Post Office. He died unmarried in 1784. When the title became extinct, his sister's son, Nicholas Lechmere, assumed the name Charlton. Massachusetts Lieutenant Governor Spencer Phipps's daughter married Richard Lechmere of the Lechmere-Charlton line. It is due to this connection that the governor honored the Charlton family by naming the new town after them in 1775. This portrait of Sir Francis is by Sir Joshua Reynolds and descended in the Lechmere family of Hanley Castle in Herefordshire.

The John Spurr House. Spurr's fame was his participation in the Boston Tea Party as a youth. He married Mercy Dunbar and moved to Charlton to oversee his father-in-law's extensive landholdings. Spurr added the Federal style front structure to an earlier crude building about 1806.

The Federated Church of Charlton was the result of a merger of the Calvinistic Congregational Church and the Universalist/Unitarian Church. This church on Main Street was destroyed in a spectacular fire on Christmas Day 1939. The structure in this photo is the new church, dedicated in 1941.

After a disastrous fire destroyed the Universalist church and the wooden, two-story combination school and high school next door, the Town of Charlton allotted the sum of $32,740 to build a new school and high school. This picture, taken in 1923, shows the newly completed brick building, much needed and appreciated by students and citizens of the town.

In 1949, the Town of Charlton borrowed $210,000 to add two wings to the 1923 high school. This same year, the town closed one-room schools in Districts 2, 4 and 6, a great leap forward for students who had been attending the old schools. This picture, taken in 1951, shows the two new additions. The building is now the George McKinstry III Municipal Building, senior center and Chip-In headquarters.

The General Salem Towne House was located where the same style of building now houses the Southbridge Savings Bank. Salem Towne built this large house in 1796. What an impressive structure in those times! Through the years, the house became somewhat tarnished and worn. In 1954, the building was taken down and rebuilt at Old Sturbridge Village, where today it is interpreted as a gentleman farmer's estate.

The Worcester and Southbridge Street Railway's luxurious resort hotel, the Overlook, was built in 1903 to serve wealthy patrons who arrived in a private trolley car called "Huguenot." After only eighteen months of operation, the hotel was forced into receivership under clouds of embezzlement by the manager. The Grand Lodge of Masons purchased the vacant hotel in 1908 as a retirement home for Masons. The Overlook Hotel was the heart of the property purchased by the Grand Lodge of Masons.

The Massachusetts Masons purchased, along with the vacant Overlook Hotel, the former Otis Farnum farm. The boss farmer oftentimes lived here. At one time, Farnum ran a tavern in this house. It is now privately owned.

It's spring, May 1952. Certainly life was simpler; the pace slower. The town of Charlton was mostly a farming community, with textile mills at Charlton City. This view was taken at the south end of the common.

Chairman of the Board of Selectmen Robert E. Brogna (right) and Bicentennial Chairman William L. Walker accept the official National Bicentennial Flag in front of town hall, as Selectmen Leonard Haebler looks on. April 17, 1975.

Charlton Women's Club, 1936–37, wearing old wedding gowns. *From left to right, back row*: Dorothy (Cook) Seifert, Evelyn (Davidson) Simpson, Rosalyn Oliver, Agnes Lunn, Florence Bates, Ruth Anderson, Doris Smith, Dorothy Truesdell, Kathleen Harris and Jean Harris. *Middle row*: Arlene (Hammond) Whitney, Dorothy Mahan, Alva Bond, Q.K. Barrett, Anna (Hammond) Miller, Merle Wilder and Laura (Bond) Truscott. *Front row*: Jean Mushroe, Q.K. Barrett's daughter and Mural (Davis) Farr.

Charlton High School, class of 1928. *From left to right, back row*: Willard Osborn, Laurier Maynard and Merton Barnes. *Middle row*: Edith Anderson, Selma Piehl, Katheryn Ball, Hazel Ray, Evelyn Bradley and Mary Cavanaugh. *Front row*: Mildred Mahan, Ella Clark, Pauline Smolen, Anita Langway and Eileen Forkey. Missing from photo is Lowell Davis.

William H. Dexter, a Charlton native, built and then donated the handsome town hall to the citizens of Charlton in 1905. It was built on the site of the fire-destroyed Belleview House Hotel on the common. Folks gather on the lawn for the traditional band concert as part of the Old Home Day festivities in this 1937 photo.

Captain William H. King and his wife are pictured at their home on Main Street, Charlton Center. Captain King served the Union cause during the Civil War, and after discharge, he came home to Charlton to a life of farming. He was involved in GAR veteran activities in Charlton and Southbridge. He lived to a couple of months shy of one hundred years and was a well-respected Charlton icon. Circa 1912.

Students from the Charlton Intermediate School were asked to write essays on the life of Dr. William T.G. Morton, Charlton's most illustrious citizen. Dr. Morton banished pain from the operating table with his use of ether in a surgical procedure. Winners read their compositions to this appreciative audience gathered in the auditorium of Dexter Memorial Hall, October 17, 1975.

This is the store at Charlton Center during the time Clarence H. Knight owned it. In front is a two-cylinder International truck. The engine is located under the seat. Clarence Knight was postmaster at Charlton Center from 1904 to 1916. He was also a dealer for International and Ford cars and trucks. Later, he moved to Southbridge.

It has been snowing in Charlton, and this picture proves it. Most of the buildings seen here are still standing, although their complexions have changed. The Congregational church can be seen in the distance. It burned down on Christmas Day 1939 and was replaced by the present Federated Church. Directly to the right is Knight's store, and beyond it, not shown, is Dexter Town Hall. Circa 1910.

In the Labor Day parade, featuring the 220th anniversary of the town of Charlton, the Charlton Boy Scouts won a trophy for most work done on a float. September 2, 1975.

On Labor Day 1975, this stand was set up on the common for Old Home Day and the bicentennial celebration. At that time, it was perhaps the only food-service booth available. Who do you know in the photo?

Cemeteries are not particularly high on the selection list for publication, but we could not resist including this fall scene at the Old Bay Path Cemetery, Charlton Center. The building at the right is the old hearse storage shed.

Charlton's handsome Civil War monument was dedicated to the thirty-two men who died while in the service of their country. The monument is a gift of William H. Dexter, who, five years later, built and gave to the town the brick town hall, later the town library, directly behind the monument.

Russell and Robert Davis, twin brothers, operated the up-to-date "Red Gate Farm," where Arnie's Auto Body is presently located on Center Depot Road. They ran the farm, milked the cows, processed the milk and delivered it. Circa 1947.

We don't know who this is with such a fine-looking team of horses and wagon. We do know that the picture was taken at Charlton Center. With this team, a stop at the corner gas station wasn't necessary. In any event, you needed a barn, hay and grain, a shovel and a measure of patience to take a ride.

The Charlton Town Pound is located on Mugget Hill Road, near the Bay Path Cemetery. In the very early days of Charlton, nearly everyone had farm animals. Often, the animals strayed onto the property of others, becoming a nuisance. The town pound was the place where the stray animals were taken until redeemed by their owners for a fee.

Going east from Charlton Center, the trolley line used to run along the right-hand side of Old Worcester Road. This view shows the trolley tracks looking east at the location of a siding, named Glenmere, where trolley cars met or passed each other. The sign on the pole reads, "PRIVATE WAY DANGEROUS." Circa 1911.

The early morning soapbox race was held at Charlton Center. Sergeant Ronald Denault of the Charlton Police Department is on duty near the finish line. This was all part of the Old Home Day and bicentennial celebration. September 2, 1975.

Looking south from the Charlton Town Hall's cupola, the Weld Tavern can be seen, and the steeple of the Federated Church is visible in the center of the picture. Beyond are Dresser Hill and the town of Dudley.

Charlton High School, 1920–21. *From left to right, bottom row*: Leo Fitzgerald, Leo Langway, Ethel Turner, Lucy Lincoln, Agnes Abell, Ruhamah Hammond, Mary Hammond, Marion Bond, Albert Smith, Burton Field, Walter Barnard, Harry Bond and William Gillespie. *Top row*: Eleanor Hollis, Ruth Hunt, Florence Sullivan, Helen Bond, Lucy Stevens, Evelyn Gale, Grace Clark, Florence Moulton, Carolyn Bacon, Helen Grady, Althea Lincoln, Elsie Stone, Hazel Darling, Edwin Russell and Herbert Gale.

Members of the Charlton High School class of 1959 are seen here on their way to New York City and Washington, D.C., on their senior class trip. *Left to right*: Caroline Jenkins, Priscilla Lavigne, Mary Cook and Trudy McGlinchy. In back on the left are John Chambers and Donald Sullivan, teachers who chaperoned the students on this exciting adventure.

After the disastrous flood of 1955 (caused by back-to-back downpours) wreaked havoc in New England, the Army Corps of Engineers was authorized to construct a series of holding reservoirs to control the major streams by regulating the flow of water backed up in the reservoirs. Buffumville Dam, shown here, straddles the Charlton/Oxford town line. The dam has regulated waters in the Little River system since it was dedicated in 1958.

Tiberri's Corner is where the Center Depot Road crosses Route 20. The house partially shown on the right was demolished, along with LaMountain's gas station, to make room for the CVS Pharmacy. The building to the left was built as the Mapleside Restaurant, but later on it was called the Jolly Dolly.

Charlton's seventy-ninth annual Old Home Day coincided nicely with the bicentennial celebration on September 2, 1975. As the float reads, "Happy Birthday Charlton."

The earliest record of this house at 13 Main Street is in an 1813 deed to John Pratt. John Spurr, participant in the Boston Tea Party, owned all the land on the west side of Main Street, which he divided into lots and sold on the common to prospective buyers.

William Weld built this structure on Charlton Common about 1804 and operated it as a tavern for many years. David Craig succeeded Mr. Weld as tavern keeper, and the structure became known as "Craig's Hall." The large hall in the ell was the location for town meetings, Masonic meetings and religious services. This southerly view shows the large ell and connected barn that were later removed. Today, the building houses a number of apartments, earning it the name "the beehive."

Before the Massachusetts Turnpike opened in 1957, Route 20 was the major highway between Boston and New York City and points west. The road provided opportunities for business establishments to flourish. The Blue Bird Tourist home, an early motel, provided cabins for travelers to spend the night. When the turnpike opened, Route 20 became a ghost road, and most business ventures languished.

Good ol' summertime. Amelia Abell (front center) doesn't look too happy flanked by Robert and Leland Baker. Alvah and Lewis King are behind them. The picture was taken in front of the new Main Street home of town doctor Abell about 1912.

Varanus Johnson moved from Old Worcester Road to Charlton Common in 1872. He built this house, which is a copy of the new Congregational parsonage at the south end of the common.

The streetcar service reached Charlton in 1902–03. The trolley waiting station was at the Overlook, the resort hotel built by the trolley company. This postcard view shows the station after its acquisition by the Grand Lodge of Masons in 1908. The waiting station is the only remaining interurban station on its original site in Massachusetts.

This Federal-period house was built by Nelson McIntire on H.K. Davis Road in 1798. It was moved to this site at 18 Main Street at an early date, at which time a long ell and a barn were added. The early town library was first housed here. The house has been known as the Shea place. In the 1950s, Mr. Shea pastured his horse on the common; he was the last to do so.

The John Haven House, 17 Main Street. In this 1820 house lived the Reverend John Haven, the longest settled minister of the Universalist church and an avid historian. The Reverend Haven produced a history of the church, a history of the cemeteries and a report of the events of the nation's centennial celebrations in Charlton.

Mail delivery, 1903 style. George Emmons Bartlett found it easier to load the mail bags into a carriage for delivery to the Clarence Knight store from the trolley stop at Charlton Center. Mr. Knight was postmaster, and he hired Mr. Bartlett to collect the twice-daily mail delivery from the trolley and bring it the quarter mile to the post office at his store.

In 1749, Nathan Macintire (McIntire) purchased the land on which he built his house on Bond Road. Nathan was one of Charlton's minutemen, who responded to the 1776 alarm. The house features fine examples of wall painting and stenciling. The southwest bedchamber walls are painted in an overall display of vines and flowers that has been much copied.

Summer home of Rufus B. Dodge on Dodge Lane, circa 1910. The Dodge family was long active in Charlton affairs. They were businessmen and quarrymen in the south part of town. Rufus summered here during his tenure as mayor of Worcester.

Grizzly Adams, noted mountain man and wild animal tamer with P.T. Barnum's Circus, is buried in Bay Path Cemetery. Grizzly, noted for his ability to tame wild animals, suffered a mortal wound from one of his grizzly bears, and upon his death, he was returned to the family plot for burial. The historical commission placed the memorial stone on his grave.

When the trolley route was laid out to Charlton in 1902, several obstacles had to be overcome, chief of which was the deep rock cut east of Charlton Center. Italian laborers blasted through the ledge and finished it off with picks and sledgehammers, earning the name "Hammerock" for the waiting place built nearby.

NORTHSIDE/DODGE

Two miles north of the Center Village is Northside, or, as it was called in early times, North Charlton. This village developed in the late eighteenth and early nineteenth century into the leading business area in Charlton. Most of the village is located in the Gore, a wedge-shaped piece of land lying on Charlton's northern border. Because Charlton's small size made it unlikely to be able to carry on the business of a municipality, the Gore land abutting the town of Charlton was annexed in 1757. The Gore lands had been divided into three-hundred-acre "farms" and were sold by the Massachusetts General Court to individuals beginning in 1723.

Among the early settlers in the Gore were the Tucker, Hammond and Wheelock families. Jonathan Wheelock built his house in 1735 on 150 acres given to him by his father. The deed read, "For the love and affection I have for my son." Besides farming, Wheelock earned a livelihood as a tavern keeper. Upon his death in 1783, his only child, Eli, assumed the tavern stand. On the stream nearby, Wheelock established a distillery. The demand for spirits and beer increased, and Wheelock's business flourished. The Reverend Peter Whitney, in his *History of Worcester County* (1790), wrote: "on the stream below there is a gin mill, brewery, malthouse, and corn mill in which he carries on each branch of the business to his and the public's benefit." Wheelock's success allowed him to partner with Leonard Morey to build a large tavern house nearby, known as Rider Tavern.

The highlight of the tavern was the 1824 visit of the Marquis de Lafayette. With completion of the rival Central Turnpike, followed by the opening of the railroad two miles away, traffic dwindled. By 1842, the tavern reverted to a two-family dwelling. The once elegant building went through a series of owners and tenants who made few changes, preserving the structure for the day when its restoration would reveal its original beauty. The roof was raised about the time the tavern was closed. In September 1938, New England was a victim of the fiercest hurricane in recorded history. Winds of 130 miles per hour were recorded, along with torrential rain. The method of roof construction used on the Rider Tavern made it highly susceptible to such a storm. The tavern was originally built with a nearly flat roof. Undoubtedly, maintenance problems caused the roof to be raised to its present hip shape about 1840.

Workers cut the former roof rafters and used them to construct the hip-shaped roof, only resting them on every fourth pair of rafters. The hurricane wind lifted the roof off like a hat. Winter came, and no repairs were done to the damages. The Culver family rented the west side of the tavern at that time. Mr. Culver was tired of going up to the attic to shovel snow out of the windows before it melted. When a thaw did come, water dripped down through the floors, and no matter how many pans he collected, they could not catch the drips. In desperation, Mr. Culver simply drilled one-inch holes in the floor and drained the water to the dirt cellar.

The area around Wheelock's was developing into a village. The local brooks provided the waterpower for a number of businesses, and the newly completed Worcester and Stafford Turnpike offered easy access to the markets east and west. A tannery was in early operation here. A scythe shop powered by a triphammer, a hatter, a mechanic and several blacksmiths were located in Northside. A Baptist church and a Universalist church served the residents' spiritual needs, while two schools and two stores provided for their other needs.

The town's activity centered on the Worcester and Stafford Turnpike, which ran through the village. In 1839, the railroad was built two miles north of Rider's Tavern, and in the 1840s, a new and more convenient turnpike was built five miles south of the village. Travelers who once patronized the W&S now took alternate routes. When the turnpike ceased operations, the village languished and returned to its rural condition.

Downstream from Northside, Tavern and Wheelock's Brooks join to form Little River at the village of Millward, later Dodge. Here was the first mill site—the Marble brothers' scythe shop. The river forms a deep gorge, a natural site for the water-powered triphammer used for shaping scythes. Later, the mill site housed the Hayward pencil shop of Sylvester Hayward, who learned the trade in the Thoreau pencil shop in Concord. Farther down the river is Pike's Pond or Downey's Reservoir, dammed to store water for the mills downstream. Continuing downriver, we pass the breached site of Job Rutter's grist- and sawmill, later Towers. At the Hammond Hill Road bridge, called Pike's Bridge, we come to the lower gorge of Little River. At this site, Pike built the first saw- and gristmill. Later, he expanded into the manufacture of shoddy cloth. Twice his mill burned, and twice it was rebuilt. Still farther along were the mills of Forbes Dodge, W.H. Young, Zenas Grover and J.H. Davidson. A sizeable village grew up around the mills to include a store, four schools, a chapel and the area's poor farm. Two taverns dispensed refreshments to travelers. The Worcester and Stafford Turnpike, and later trolleys, provided access to the village. One by one, the mills closed. By World War II, the last of Dodge's mills had closed. The post office closed in 1954, ending the use of the common phrase "goin' down Dodge" by folks traveling to that part of Charlton.

The village was called Millward for the many mills located there. When the growth of Millward required better postal facilities, to save residents from having to travel five miles to the Center Village post office, Forbes Dodge petitioned the postal service for a post office. The name "Millward" was on the petition, but it was rejected by postal authorities because of its similarity to other offices with the prefix "Mill." "Put Dodge instead," said the elder Mr. Dodge. It was accepted, and thus the village became Dodge.

Dodge Chapel was organized in 1901 as the Church of Christ in Charlton by several people wishing to have a place of worship in Dodge Village. The effort was short-lived; by 1905, the chapel was vacant. The Helping Hand Society acquired the place thereafter, adding a steeple and expanding the building.

District 2 School, 1933–34. 1. Edward Gouin, 2. Robert Bostrom, 3. Bruce Lamprey, 4. Carl Blomberg, 5. Gordon Fountain, 6. Ruth Turskey, 7. George Lamprey Jr. and 8. Curtis Smith.

This picture looks east toward the future Northside Road bridge, which will cross over the brand-new Massachusetts Turnpike. All the buildings in this scene are long gone, as this picture was taken very early in the construction of the road. The home in the foreground belonged to Bruce Lamprey, who later erected a new home on Stafford Street.

Like most towns, Charlton had several villages, and at one time, Dodge was one of them. If, years ago, someone said, "Get out of Dodge," it meant something. Today, not many would understand. This view shows the Dodge Post Office and Olson's store. The post office closed on April 30, 1954; no longer would the Dodge postmark be sent.

Located on Carroll Hill Road, this house was the birthplace of Dr. Martin Rutter, prominent in the early days of the Methodist Church in New England. It was also the birthplace of Jerome Marble, who made his mark in business and banking. In 1877, he established Worcester Excursion Car Company, using luxurious, custom-built railroad palace cars for hunting trips out West.

In 1986, Conrail started to single track the old Boston & Albany railroad between Framingham and Selkirk, New York. This picture, looking east from the Stafford Street bridge, shows the work in progress. If you look farther along the roadbed, you can see the double track still in place. Directly in front is a tamper, a track machine that forces the ballast under the ties and levels the track.

The Jacob Davis House is on Carroll Hill Road in Dodge Village. Davis acquired over two hundred acres of Charlton land, upon which he built this house. In 1786, Jacob mortgaged his property and moved to Vermont, where he purchased three townships. He helped organize the town of Montpelier, in which he was the first settler. Davis returned to Charlton and successfully recruited settlers for his towns. He led the way, walking the distance in the winter and drawing sleds loaded with their household goods. Davis, however, died in paupers' jail in 1814.

In 1954, Pauline and Otto Hultgren opened a tearoom in their home, which grew to a full service restaurant. The old barn was remodeled, using knotty pine cut from trees on the property, and a fieldstone fireplace was added to the décor. One could order a dinner of native rabbit for $2.25. Rhoda Cooper, with her sister-in-law, Dorothy Fales, were waitresses at the Little Valley Farm Restaurant, which operated at the 50 Northside Road site from 1954 to 1967.

The neighbors gathered at the Prunier home on Prenier Drive to repair the roads in District 4 with the road machine, drawn by two teams. Each spring, after mud season, when the dirt roads dried out, the road surface required grading and repairs. Today's "Prenier" is the Yankee variation of the French *Prunier*.

Few men nowadays can handle a yoke of oxen. Dr. Marc Ledoux clears roots after breaking up the field opposite Rider Tavern for planting.

The oldest house in Northside Village is this house at 273 Stafford Street. It was built by Jonathan Wheelock on 150 acres of land given to him by his father, "for love and affection I have for my son Jonathan," in 1735. The original house was a simple Cape-type dwelling, to which a second story was added. In the front room of this house, Jonathan, and later his son Eli, operated a tavern.

Chauncy Pike proudly poses for a photo in his right-hand steering-wheeled car in front of the family home on Hammond Hill Road in Dodge.

Smith Road takes its name from the Smith farm, seen here in a 1954 photo. The elderly, bachelor Smith brothers farmed here and tended the orchard until infirmities caused them to retire to a care facility. The house was rented out when a fire destroyed it in 1968. The orchard gave its name to the subdivision Applewood, which now occupies the site.

Jesse Smith built this center-chimney house on the new Worcester and Stafford Turnpike about 1810. Smith was philanthropically minded. He donated the bell for the Northside Baptist Church, established a fund for students and donated land for a cemetery.

In this 1950 picture, we see the John Hammond Farm. The Hammonds were early settlers in County Gore, which later became part of Charlton. Mr. Hammond wore many hats in Charlton, as selectman, highway superintendent and Old Home Day organizer, among others.

Ebenezer Hammond built this house in 1800. The house at 231 Stafford Street features a "Haven" doorway, built by housewright John A. Haven, that can be identified by the use of the architectural embellishments of heavy, rusticated sides and keystone lintel. The barn in the photo burned in 1969 and was replaced. The farm was known as Indian Mortar Farm from the ancient mortar stone found here. After World War II, John Cook, who was the last Charlton farmer to use only horses in his farm work, acquired the farm.

The old Worcester & Stafford Turnpike route (right) is easily seen in this view. Opened in 1810, the turnpike brought prosperity to the Charlton villages through which it passed. The building of the railroad and the opening of a rival turnpike doomed the W&S. Turnpike operations ceased in 1843, and the road became a public highway, today's Stafford Street.

Ancient slate gravestones mark the resting place of Captain Jonathan Tucker and his wife in the woods on the three hundred acres of land the Tucker family acquired in 1730.

The Northside Road bridge of the Massachusetts Turnpike is in the early stages of construction in this 1955 photo. The '55 Ford, we assume, was the photographer's.

Senator Edward M. Kennedy spoke at the Dr. William T.G. Morton Commemoration program at the Gilmore home, at 5 Cemetery Road, on October 16, 1975. This was part of the bicentennial celebration. Dr. Morton was the first to use ether in an operation, earning him the title "the man who banished pain from the operating table." As a youth, Morton lived in this house.

Fun could be had after the snowstorm of February 1980 piled the snow midway up the windows and a tunnel was dug to the front door. Eric and Shelley Hultgren enjoy their tunnel in this picture.

This backyard view over Boot Shop Pond from Cemetery Road shows the Mary Waters House (1796) on the left, with the Ebenezer Hammond House (1800) in the distance.

Although most farmers had given up the use of horses for their farm work, a few men, who had a love for old-time farming, continued to use them on the job. Donald Stone and his team cut grass at Little Valley Farm on Northside Road in this 1981 photo.

What could be more fun than tree climbing? Shelley Hultgren is on the ladder, hoping to join Craig Manfield and Eric Hultgren on the limbs.

The Mary Waters House is located on Stafford Street in Northside Village. Israel Waters, a local tanner, built this house for his mother in 1796 on part of his property. The handsome door surround is typical of John A. Haven, local housewright, with its rusticated sides and keystone lintel. Leslie and Minnie Olney ran an antique shop here for many years, recently followed by Stephen and Bonnie Clark.

Every autumn, the Charlton Historical Society sponsors "History Day," a celebration of Charlton's past, with open houses, wagon rides, craft demonstrations and reenactments, such as these 1812 militiamen in front of Rider Tavern.

Ronald Fountain built this house on Dodge Road in the 1930s as a newlywed. The Massachusetts Turnpike Authority's design for the toll road put the house in the path of the highway. In 1955, the house was placed on a truck and moved across the field to a new site at 1 Millward Road.

A few families carried on the tradition of lighting the Christmas tree with live candles. Carl Hultgren admires the Christmas wonder of the illuminated tree in his 50 Northside Road home in 1984 .

The George Camp Chapel in the Northside Cemetery was built by Mrs. Lila Camp over the grave of her only child.

The District 2 (Northside) Schoolhouse in winter garb creates a perfect picture. Classes ended in 1949. Today it is the Charlton Cultural Center.

The ice was perfect for skating on Hultered Pond for Eric, Linnea and Shelley Hultgren and friend Teddy in their kicksled.

The Dennis House is one of the oldest in Charlton. There was already a house on the property when Ezra McIntire sold it in 1774 to Isaac Dennis. The Oscar Anderson family, father then son, lived here for many years. In this snapshot, Oscar Sr. stands outside his home, located today at 38 Northside Road.

The former Hyde place, Hammond Hill Road in Dodge, about 1925. At that time, it was the home of Harry Waldron, his brothers and family. It was operated as a rooming house for men who worked in the Pike and Dodge mills in Dodge. In later years, the barn and ell were removed, and the house became derelict and was torn down.

This page: The Reverend Caleb Curtis, the first minister in Charlton in 1762, built the old Manse or Eastman Homestead at 92 Northside Road. The established church (Congregational) voted to call the Reverend Curtis as their minister, and he chose to build his house two miles from the church. The simple Cape-style house was the home of Reverend Curtis until his death in 1802, when the son of the Baptist minister, Reverend Boomer, purchased it. Since then, five generations of Eastmans have lived and farmed here. The removal of the central chimney and raising the roof in 1940 to accommodate an apartment has altered the house. The photos show a before and after view.

Rider Tavern is one of the ten most architecturally significant structures in Massachusetts, as recognized by the Massachusetts Historical Commission. Built in 1797–99 at 253 Stafford Street by Eli Wheelock and partner Leonard Morey, Rider Tavern once featured a roof garden and running water. Upon the untimely death of Mr. Wheelock, brothers William and Isaiah Rider purchased the tavern. The Riders presided over an expanded popular inn, on the recently opened Worcester and Stafford Turnpike. Stagecoaches called at the tavern, and the Riders were the genial hosts to the drovers and wagoners who frequented the barroom.

The award-winning restoration of Rider Tavern began when historian Richard Green purchased the building in 1967 and transferred the title to the Charlton Historical Society in 1975.

The restored Rider Tavern is probably the most outstanding Federal Period Inn in New England.

The Massachusetts Turnpike was one of the major factors in the development of Charlton since the building of the railroad. Businesses, which were almost entirely highway oriented, found themselves devoid of traffic. Overnight travelers on Route 20 from Boston and points east to New York now traveled the new toll road. Ten filling stations were reduced to two, while overnight facilities for travelers dwindled from six to two.

This welcoming path leads through the Widow Rider's garden to the door of the Rider Tavern.

SOUTH CHARLTON

The area south and west of Charlton Center and Route 20 is known collectively as South Charlton. Barefoot, Phillipsdale, Lyons Corner, Dresser Hill, Hell's County, Lelandville, Buffumville, Community Park or Morseville are names that old-time locals still use to describe the residential areas. These areas have always possessed a character and charm all their own, recounted in stories over the years. Areas like Mystic Grove, Glen Grove and the lesser-known Community Park were 1930s developments of summer cottages and camps around the lakes and ponds. Small-time industries coexisted with two significant businesses—the manufacture of swords, ramrods and knives; and the quarrying of granite at Lelandville. Dresser Hill was a place of small industries early on. Barefoot was the section in which the men attended annual military muster, without shoes. Hell's County is named, perhaps, for its wilder behavior (you can draw your own conclusions). Enjoy South Charlton for its lakes and ponds, hills and dales. It doesn't take a backseat to anyone.

The character and uniqueness of the people is well illustrated in stories—or, if you wish, tales—of the life and times in South Charlton.

Mrs. Devlin's Disappearance

This is the story of Ann Devlin, who lived on the south end of Haggerty Road in South Charlton. Pictured in this chapter is her humble home, from which she wandered and to which she never returned. Her disappearance was never solved. Around 1904, many people walked to and from their destinations. Ann Devlin was a lady who seemed to walk everywhere to visit friends and neighbors on a daily basis. One spring evening, Ann was returning to her home after a visit in Dudley. The path she followed skirted the western shore of Baker Pond. Her walk coincided with a rather severe thunder and lightning storm. She did not arrive home that night, and search parties were unable to find even a small clue to her disappearance. A few years later, some skeletal remains of a human were found on Christmas Tree Island at the south end of Baker Pond. Mr. Devlin, Ann's husband, was able to identify his wife's remains by the clothes she wore and a ring he had given her. We will never know what happened to her on that terrible night.

School Days and Cows

Back in the period from 1919 to 1922, when the coauthor's mother, Althea Lincoln, was attending Charlton High School, things were different. In the morning, after getting ready for school and eating breakfast at her home on Ramshorn Road, the next job was to hook up the horse and wagon. Once that was done, Althea drove to Charlton Center to the horse sheds in back of the Federated Church, where she boarded the horse for the day. When she got back home, it was time to round up the cows and get them back into the barn for milking. Because Althea's father did not properly maintain their fences, some bovines wandered all over the place. Often, it would take a couple of hours to round up the strays. Althea often said how she hated this cow "round-up job" the most.

The Advent Church dedicated this building on May 23, 1869, making this the oldest church building in town. For many years, the church was painted brown and was known locally as "the Little Brown Church in the Vale."

For most of Charlton's existence, scenes like this view of the Baylies Farm on Dresser Hill Road was an everyday sight. At one time, cows and horses outnumbered residents.

You are traveling north on Carpenter Hill Road, looking ahead at the Carrington place. Across from the house is Snake Hill Road. Take a look at that typical Charlton barn, perhaps never painted. One might wonder why. The answer is: it costs money. July 9, 1953.

This 1910 picture of Roy Burlingame and his bride, Bessie Stone, was probably posed in the photographer's studio, complete with automobile. The Burlingame family lived in South Charlton, and many descendants still reside there.

Over eight hundred people attended the bicentennial picnic at the YMCA's Camp Foskett on July 20, 1975. Shown is one of the many activities held during the day on the shore of the South Charlton Reservoir.

Ebenezer Foskett of Stoneham settled in the western part of Oxford in 1739 on what is now Daniels Road. He was one of the founding fathers of the town of Charlton and an early selectman. A long line of Foskett descendants have lived in South Charlton on land that is now Camp Foskett. This interesting picture was taken at the family homestead in 1912. It was the fiftieth anniversary of Dan and Milia Foskett.

Charlton celebrated at the bicentennial picnic at Camp Foskett, Daniels Road, South Charlton. The Charlton Junior Firefighters sold refreshments. This picture shows Mr. Baylies paying Mr. Jeacopello as Charlton fire chief Carrington helps out.

Nine generations of Fosketts have occupied this property, ending with Lindsey Foskett, his son Edwin and his two daughters, Elaine and Eleanor. The property was later sold to the YMCA in Southbridge, and all the buildings were removed. At this site, Camp Foskett was built along the shore of the South Charlton Reservoir.

The Nathaniel McIntire place is the only old house located on McIntire Road. Here, Lewis McIntire, later the town undertaker, was born. Paris Rich also lived here. Elisha Rich gave a plot of land, thirty feet by forty feet, for a schoolhouse in the district called Lyons Corner. The house has been added to and the brick wall has been covered the stucco. For several years, the Dean family erected greenhouses filled with hydroponically grown tomatoes and cucumbers. In this process, plants are grown without soil, and the nourishment is supplied by adding nutrients to the water.

Prindle Hill farmhouse stands on the crest of Prindle Hill, named for Guy Prindle, who owned the place for many years. Robert Craig built this fine example of a Cape-style house on 110 acres by 1769. Guy Prindle was not only a farmer, but also his entrepreneurial spirit led him to run a general store and publish a series of postcards of Charlton views. Later, owners opened the house as a bed-and-breakfast and also ran a country store.

James Reynolds came from Dudley to purchase this farm in 1818. It has remained in the family ever since. This 1952 scene shows the farmhouse and barn complex at 30 Reynolds Road, now the home of Marion Reynolds. Her father and mother, Lewis and Lena, raised eight children on the farm. For many years, they bottled milk on the farm, and Mr. Reynolds delivered the milk in Southbridge.

Charles Gale lived in this old house at 17 Gale Road when this photo was taken about 1900.

In this wintry scene, the snowdrifts are piled up to a depth of seven feet, as measured by John Hunt alongside the 1950 Ford on Dresser Hill Road during this February 1961 storm.

Lowell Baylies poses with the airfield wind vane he made for his landing field at 189 Dresser Hill Road. Lowell's father, Lester, was the first airplane pilot in Charlton and constructed the landing field on his farm.

In this 1949 snapshot, Ralph Loomis is collecting eggs from his flock of Rhode Island Red hens. Parts of his henhouse were constructed from lumber salvaged from the collapsed District 10 schoolhouse.

Maple Rock Farm is located at 61 Harrington Road. This house was built about 1822 adjacent to the ancient Bay Path aboriginal trail. It ran from the bay at Boston to the Connecticut River and was traveled by the settlers of early towns in the Connecticut Valley.

The old knife shop. It is said that this building was the site of the first manufacturing of knives by the Harrington family, which evolved into the well-known Russell Harrington Knife Company, now located in Southbridge.

Haying on the Phillips Farm off Harrington Road is pictured here. This was a common scene at one time in Charlton. You cut the hay, let it dry, rake it up into windrows and then pitch it on the wagon. When the wagon is loaded, you head to the barn, all the time hoping it doesn't rain.

John H. Stevens was the only Charlton farmer who preferred mules to horses in his farm work. In this view, Stevens rides the sickle mowing machine behind his mules as he cuts hay.

As we look back on the history of Charlton, what could be more symbolic of the town's farming past than this fall scene on Dresser Hill Farm. That's Oliver May on the Allis-Chalmers tractor.

Edwin Phillips operated a sawmill and gristmill, in addition to farming, on the Southbridge Road (now Route 169). To provide additional waterpower for these enterprises, he dammed Cedar Swamp, forming today's Prindle Pond. For many years, Mr. Phillips was Charlton's largest taxpayer.

The Phillips Farm on Harrington Road was perhaps the most prosperous farm in the area. Edwin Phillips not only engaged in farming, but he also had interests in manufacturing and in lumbering operations. A large saw timber log is being dragged to the Phillips sawmill by a sturdy team in this circa 1910 photo.

Annual road scraping was done in each district after the spring thaw by the neighbors in that district. In this postcard view, neighboring farmers are scraping and grading Sampson Road; in later years, an oil and tar mix alleviated this annual necessity.

During the early days of this century, Everett Phillips delivered milk to his customers from the milk can to the patron's own personal container. This picture, staged to simulate the way it was done, shows Everett and his wife, Edith, in front of their home on Harrington Road. Circa 1908.

Eleven men were employed by Edwin Phillips at his portable sawmill. This mill was set up to harvest the timber in Cedar Meadow.

Charlton was certainly quite rural in nature at the turn of the century. Almost every household operated a small farm, and this provided most of the necessities of life. This 1905 picture shows the Lincoln family in South Charlton.

A hiker pauses to enjoy the peaceful scene at the lower dam on the west branch of the Little River, not far from Lelandville Road.

Charlton is often remembered for its large dairy farms. During this era, many smaller family farms existed, each with a few cows, chickens and pigs, as well as a garden. This 1945 picture shows the hay pick-up in South Charlton on the Lincoln Farm.

This is a moving tribute to rural Schoolhouse #6. It is on the move to a new location, where it will be part of a private residence in another part of Charlton. Since it was built, it had occupied that same spot of land at the junction of Freeman, Ramshorn, Coburn, Haggerty and No. 6 Schoolhouse Roads. This picture shows the school passing the brick house on Freeman Road during the 1979 move.

Camp Wamsutta, on Anderson Drive at Colicum Pond, was earlier known as Idlewild Farm. Mr. and Mrs. Samuel Sleeper operated a Jewish summer camp on the shore of the pond, which was incorporated into Buffumville Reservoir when the latter was dammed.

Another of Charlton's rural scenes is shown in this snapshot of the stone arch bridge over McKinstry Brook in winter dress.

A typical bucolic Charlton scene is captured in this photo. The Edwin Baylies farm on the north slope of Dresser Hill was settled about 1780 and was active well into the twentieth century.

CHARLTON CITY

The term "city," in Charlton context, means that the locality is as busy as a city. In the past, as well as now, this area of Charlton was the foremost village, with mills and other enterprises strung tightly along Cady Brook. The history of Charlton City is a history of its mills. The three woolen mills of the Akers & Taylor Company and the Ashworth Company were the mainstays of Charlton City. Countless smaller businesses, such as the Prouty Wire Company, depended, in the early years, on the waterpower supplied by the brooks and the reservoirs and millponds upstream. It is said that the first mill in the city was in operation as early as 1760 at the Carpenter's mill site. Over the years, most of these sites had sawmill or gristmill operations—necessities in those times. In 1806, Charlton City was selected as a location for a tollhouse on the new Worcester and Stafford Turnpike, an indication of the volume of traffic on that road.

The uppermost mill on Cady Brook was the Prouty wire mill. It was located just below the Massachusetts Turnpike bridge. The office building is the only remaining part of the Prouty complex, having survived the 1955 flood. Mr. Prouty built the houses on Brookfield Road, called Proutyville, for the use of millworkers. During the Depression, the mill discontinued operations, and the Prouty mill and housing were sold off. The one mile between Proutyville and Southbridge Road was crowded with various enterprises, with one mill after the other vying for water privileges along Cady Brook.

The one-hundred-acre reservoir, now called Glen Echo Lake, was built to store water for the downstream mills and to augment the flow in Cady Brook. The disastrous flood of August 1955 was the result of torrential rains, which overflowed Glen Echo and burst the dam, sending a wall of water down the brook into Charlton City, resulting in six deaths. A small stream, Spring Brook, joins Cady Brook above the former Charlton Woolen Company's upper mill. The mill, for many years, depended upon the waterpower provided by the pond on Spring Brook.

In 1878, Edward Akers acquired the upper mill privilege, called the Spring Brook privilege. This was the beginning of the business partnership of Akers & Taylor, which evolved into the firm of the Charlton Woolen Company. With the purchase of the downstream Norris privilege, the company expanded and took an active role in the development of Charlton City. Company housing was built, streets were laid out and a company store was opened. The "City" became the business center of Charlton.

The Norris privilege is the last mill site before the waters of Sibley Brook join those of Cady Brook. On Sibley Brook, Lyman Sibley built a saw- and gristmill early in the nineteenth century. By 1836, two storage reservoirs were built for the use of the mill. Merrit D. Aldrich and Reuben Walling built a large mill to process and weave woolen cloth at the earlier site. The Ashworth brothers, Thomas, James and Richard, bought the mill in 1904. A fire destroyed the mill two years later, but it was quickly rebuilt.

The arrival of the streetcar or trolley in 1903 proved a boon to the businessmen and citizens of Charlton City. Businessmen enjoyed the freight availability provided by the trolley, and the passenger cars offered fast and cheap transportation for the residents. But by 1927, the use of private cars had reduced the need for the trolley. The new highway, Route 20, passed through the village and replaced streetcar service, just as the earlier turnpike and trolley line had done. Route 20 proved to be so popular to travelers driving to New York and points west that, by midcentury, the need for relief was apparent. The opening of the Massachusetts Turnpike in 1957 reduced traffic through the village to a trickle. Many highway-dependant businesses suffered and closed. However, by the end of the twentieth century, business had rebounded, traffic had increased and the road through the "City" was rebuilt.

The lifeblood of the village of Charlton City was its woolen mills. This view is of the lower or Cady Brook mill of the Charlton Woolen Company, formerly Akers & Taylor Company, which housed the operations where the woolen cloth was dyed, sized and finished.

The Charlton Volunteer Fire Department members are posed in front of the Charlton City fire barn in this 1960 photo. *From left to right, front row*: Frank Kubesh, Herman Leschke, Arthur Bellerive, David Lawrence, Philip Divoll, Clarence Smith and Everett Beckwith Sr. *Back row*: Everett Beckwith Jr., Fred Stevens, Raymond Williams, William Emco, William Walker, Donald Stearns and Tellis Nale.

The dedication of Charlton's new $21,000 fire station on Power Station Road, Charlton City. This is a three-stall, concrete brick building, sixty feet long and forty feet deep. The picture shows, from the left, fire chief Divoll's car, the 1949 Ford truck and the World War II–era, 750-gallon "Buffalo" fire truck. The two trucks to the right are civil defense trucks. March 2, 1958.

The Roman Catholic population in Charlton was served by a mission church, Sacred Heart, located on City Depot Road, until St. Joseph's was built in 1904 on Worcester Road. This St. Joseph's Church was destroyed in a 1922 blaze. A new church was built on the Worcester Road site.

Lillian Hemminway was an avid photographer, capturing many scenes in the Charlton City area. Another cameraman caught Mrs. Hemminway and her husband, Henry, in a 1905 photo.

Henry Hemminway built this house at 4 Brookfield Road about 1910.

The uppermost mill located on Cady Brook was the George Prouty wire mill. In 1871, Prouty began the manufacture of fine card wire in this building on Brookfield Road. The white office building was the only structure to escape the destruction of the floodwaters in 1955.

The floodwaters from the torrential rain of August 11–20, 1955, caused six deaths and millions of dollars in damage, especially in the village of Charlton City. The dam at Glen Echo burst, sending a mass of water into the city. The weave room of the Charlton Woolen Company was destroyed, and the mill was damaged. Repairs were made, and a new weave room was built on the site of the destroyed company offices.

WILLIAM S. GILLESPIE

LITTLE VALLEY FARM

BOX 148 :: TEL. 64

CHARLTON CITY, MASS.

This page: We don't often think about cows and farming when Charlton City is mentioned. However, at the end of Gillespie Road in the City, William Gillespie ran the "Little Valley Farm," one of Charlton's numerous milk-producing operations. The photos show Mr. and Mrs. Gillespie at their home. An advertisement for their farm is seen below.

Charlton City Baseball Team, 1932. *From left to right, top row*: Leon Lafler, Robert Bruce, G. Beckworth, Bill Gillespie, Dan Daley, Henry Langway, Ralph Ashe, Robert Gard and Z. Poulin. *Bottom row*: T. Demarious, Arthur Bennett, Leo Daley, A. Beckworth, J. Gauthier and L. Conforti. The bat boy is Valmore Richards.

Mildred Stegenga is sorting mail in the Charlton City Post Office.

Edward Akers, mill owner, was a lover of fine horses. Here he poses with his sulky and horse on the lawn of the Methodist church.

"July 12, 1902—A new automobile arrived in Charlton Depot Tuesday for Fred S. Taylor, of Akers & Taylor. Its motive-power is electricity. Mr. Taylor has arranged so that the batteries can be charged at the Spring Brook Mill. It will run 25 miles with one charge. The machine is equipped with a six horse power motor."

—Southbridge News

This building still stands on Route 20 in Charlton City. The signs reads: "D.J. Sullivan Groceries and Provisions," but also includes the Charlton City Post Office. You could buy gas for your auto here, if you wished. In front, notice the trolley track that could take you to Southbridge or Worcester and beyond.

This page: Seen here are interesting pictures of the trolley car barn that was built at Charlton City in 1902–03. The top photo shows the barn after trolley service was abandoned in 1927. Note the house at the top left, presently owned by the Cavanaugh family and located on Masonic Home Road. The bottom photo shows the beautifully built brick car barn and the tracks going up the hill toward Charlton Center.

The waiting station for the Worcester & Southbridge Street Railway trolley is seen in this circa 1927 postcard. The barber, Mr. Dugas, and a young customer are standing on the porch. Mr. Dugas and his son, Alphonse, ran the shop for over forty years. J.W. Ryan ran a soda shop and a convenience store in part of the building, as well as selling gasoline. The building served a number of enterprises over the years, until it was torn down in 1972. The trolley tracks are in the foreground.

The parlor car "Huguenot" was put in service by the Worcester & Southbridge Street Railway to carry the wealthy clientele from Worcester's Union Station to the Overlook Hotel built on the high hill west of Charlton Center. Today's Masonic Care Facility has adopted the Overlook name.

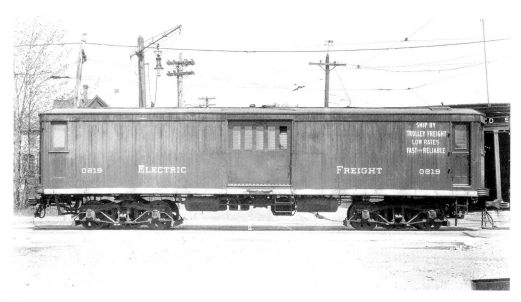

These trolley freight cars radiated in all directions out of Worcester, including Charlton. They would leave in early morning, sometimes loaded to the roof with freight. The motorman would help the car's messenger unload the car at the many stops en route to Southbridge.

August 19, 1955, was a bad and sad day in Charlton City. After a period of heavy rains, spawned by Hurricane Diane, Glen Echo Lake's dam let go, releasing a thirty-foot wall of water that devastated the area. This picture shows the remains of Gale's garage, which also housed Charlton's two fire trucks. Wisely, they had been moved to higher ground.

We are standing on Route 20 in Charlton City, looking east. Just to our left is the City Primary School. Farther along is the three-story Wilkinson's Store, which also houses the post office. Just beyond that, on the same side, is Mahan's Cottage Diner, famous for its hamburgers. Note the Tydol sign—a little back from the road and out of sight is the gas station. The steeple of St. Joseph's Church, which is next to City Grade School, is visible. Although the road looks deserted on this 1939 morning, this was the main road between Boston and New York and other points west, and it was normally crowded with autos, trucks and buses. Unfortunately, it was also frequently the scene of many accidents, sometimes fatal.

After a head-on collision between two trolleys near Morton Station Road, which resulted in the death of an employee, the two damaged cars ended up at the Charlton City car barn. Both cars caught fire in the wreck, and one of them is shown in this picture. Also shown is the backside of the car barn, a view seldom seen in photos.

On the move to Millennium Power is this huge boiler module, traveling along Route 169. A great deal of preparation is required to make this move possible from Charlton Depot to the Millenium Power plant construction site.

This schoolhouse was constructed in District 10 before 1800. The district was called Barefoot District after the unshod residents who attended the annual muster. Earliest records list the area as the Rum Hill Ward. Classes continued until 1919, after which the school building was sold for its salvage value.

Ezra Taylor settled the Mann Homestead at 100 Tinker Hall Road as early as 1783. His farm consisted of 122 acres and a dwelling. The brick house seen in the photo was built sometime later. In 1871, James Mann bought the farm, and it remains in the family today.

The Bracket place, formerly George Prouty's, is located at 30 Brookfield Road. In this 1969 photo, the two barns can be seen. They were torn down shortly after this photo was taken. R.A. Bracket and his family lived here for many years.

The firewood is stacked neatly in this 1908 view of the Thayer place on South Sturbridge Road. Irving Bennett lived here for many years.

The word to describe this picture might be progress. At the right front is the newly built power station of the trolley line. Above this, the new St. Joseph's Church, and City Grade School next door, can be seen. Look to the horizon to see the water tower at the new Overlook Hotel. To the left is the remodeled hotel; below that is the Aklor house. Circa 1903.

In the 1950s, the threat of nuclear destruction was a serious matter. The government encouraged the building of fallout shelters stocked with supplies to last for a period of time until it was safe to come out. American Optical executive George Wells, with his wife, Ruth, had this shelter built at their home, Gayville West, on Capen Road.

CHARLTON DEPOT

Charlton Depot is located four miles north of Charlton Center Village, on the main railroad line from Boston to Springfield. The village grew up after the railroad was put through in 1839. During the twentieth century, the village prospered to include stores, shoe shops, wheelwright shops, a chapel and a school. The village of Charlton Depot has had its share of fires over the last century.

On July 26, 1902, lightning destroyed the H.I. Gould Grocery and Grain store near the B&A (Boston and Albany) passenger station. The building also contained the Charlton Depot Post Office and an American Express facility. The fire began around 10:00 p.m., and whistles from two locomotives that were in the area aroused the sleeping village; by 11:00 p.m. the building was burned to the ground. Had it not been for heavy rain, other buildings would also have been lost in the fire. No fire department was available in the village to prevent, or at least attempt to contain, the fire.

In May 1922, another large fire started on a farm at the top of Curtis Hill. The farmhouse, along with its outbuildings, was totally destroyed, and the owner was badly burned. Sparks from the fire spread to other buildings in the village. Had it not been for the efforts of the Spencer and Southbridge Fire Departments, which had been summoned, and the availability of nearby water, the entire village would have been wiped out. The town of Charlton did not have a fire truck at this time.

Another disastrous fire occurred in April 1927. A house and barn were destroyed by fire near the Spencer town line when a spark from a locomotive on the nearby railroad set fire to the grass in a neighboring field. The property was known at the time as the Ward Homestead, and it contained many antiques.

During a twenty-four-hour period, Charlton experienced three major fires: the Ward fire, a destructive chimney fire at the Charlton City Hotel and a large brush fire near the Tucker Farm on Stafford Street.

About 1910, a potential train wreck was averted by a sharp-eyed Charlton citizen, who spotted a broken rail on the mainline track at Charlton Depot. Adin Bond, a young man who was lounging around the Frank Knight's Store, spotted the broken rail. He quickly realized that the fast passenger train, the "20th Century Limited," was due from the west on the same track. Galvanized into action, he found a red signal flag near the station and ran down the track in an effort to stop the high-speed train. And stop it he did, just in the nick of time, preventing a major disaster! He received a letter of commendation and a gold watch from the railroad for his heroic deed.

The village of Charlton Depot as viewed from Little Mugget Hill. Curtis Hill Road, in the center, is the only residential street connecting the old railroad depot with the former Kestigian Farm, whose large barns can be seen in the center of the photo.

The Western Railroad was built through Charlton in 1838, cutting travel time to the Eastern cities from two days to a few hours. A village soon grew up around the depot, and a post office was established in 1842. This view shows Charlton Depot, looking east to the recently built bridge. The old passenger and freight house is on the left. The large white house is the Summit House, a boardinghouse and stable.

Lauritz Nielsen, a Danish immigrant, owned the Charlton Hill Farm at 226 Brookfield Road for many years. The grape arbor offered a shady retreat for him and his wife.

Sunset Hill Farm, also known as Charlton Hill Farm, is located at 226 Brookfield Road. The house is an architectural gem featuring many classical and Federal details. Barnabas Commins is said to have built this house in 1796.

The old highway bridge that crossed the B&A Railroad tracks at Charlton Depot can be seen in the distance. The bridge was built in 1891–92 and eliminated the dangerous station crossing, where many accidents occurred involving teams and pedestrian traffic. In the early 1950s, a new bridge was built to replace the old one. At this time, the area experienced many changes in the landscape around the new bridge.

This westbound freight has topped the summit at Charlton Depot in this 1930s picture. It has been a hard pull uphill from Worcester, and the trip to Springfield will be much easier from here. Today, only one mainline track remains. Still, this continues to be a busy railroad, running about twenty-four trains per day.

The elegant Boston section of the Twentieth Century Limited is seen approaching Hammond Curve, Charlton, in the 1937 view. This train was the fastest passenger train on the New York Central, the pride of the fleet, with the Boston train continuing service until the late 1930s. It was replaced by the New England States Limited, which ran between Boston and Chicago. The New York City–Chicago Twentieth Century was in operation until 1967.

April 1934 saw the first diesel-powered train to pass through Charlton on the B&A railroad. This train was one of the earliest lightweight, streamlined passenger cars to run on America's railroads. The train belonged to the Burlington Railroad and was on a tour of the country.

In the state fire tower at Charlton Depot, the man on duty uses the "alligator" to line up, in degrees, an apparent spotting of a fire. This line, in simple terms, will correspond to a focused line on the same fire from another tower, pinpointing the location. This 70-foot tower raises the elevation to 1,080 feet, and it is still the best way to spot fires.

This 1976 view at Charlton Depot shows Conrail's welded rail train, ready to drop long strings of welded rail adjacent to the track.

Three locomotives are seen in this unusual picture taken at Charlton Depot. These locomotives are required to handle flatcars loaded with continuous welded rail for installation, to replace the older jointed rail. All are part of Conrail's extensive replacement of track through Charlton. Spring 1976.

This Conrail westbound extra freight, with 13 locomotives and 141 cars, has topped the summit at Charlton. Its destination is the large classification yard at Selkirk (Albany), New York.

Raffael (Fred) Loconto worked forty-six years for the Boston and Albany Railroad, from 1902 to 1948. He is seen at his Charlton Depot home with his grandson Peter. His son, Peter, also worked many years on the railroad. Both father and son were employed in the Maintenance of Way Department as track inspectors, a responsible and important part of railroading.

The highway department's new road grader was at work on a woodsy roadway on a warm spring morning. Longtime highway workers Walter Baylies and Joe Zinkowsky confer on the project at hand.

The machinery changes, but the job is the same. This 1912 photo shows the road scraper grading Main Street in front of Captain King's residence.

Pleasant View Farm is the name of this farm at 92 Fitzgerald Road. It was the home of the Gustafson and Nelson families. The large barns are now gone, but there remains an in-ground ice cellar, one of only two known in Massachusetts. The farm is the northerly section of the so-called Yeoman Lot, granted in 1713.

A symbol of the importance of Charlton's dairy farms can be seen in the 1920s picture of Lauritz Nielsen and his milk wagon. Mr. Nielsen's farm was located on Brookfield Road and was known as Charlton Hill Farm. If only we could go back, buy a bottle of milk and chat with Lauritz Nielsen.

What could be more fun than an ice cream cone on a hot summer day, especially if you're a kid? Hunter Lavigne and his sister, Jacquelyn, prove the point at this popular Depot location.

"Off to church in a sleigh, 1935," is the title of this snapshot. The Savoie family farmed on T. Hall Road and attended church four miles away in Charlton City. Identified in the front row, from left to right, are Irene Savoie, Antoinette Corriveau and Louisia Savoie. In the back row are Alfred Savoie, Antoine Corriveau, Edwina Savoie and Alcide Savoie.

ABOUT THE AUTHORS

William O. Hultgren has had a lifelong interest in history. This has resulted in his writing a series of historical books and monograms of local interest. A founding member of the Charlton Historical Society, where he is past president and director, Hultgren was involved in the award-winning restoration of the Rider Tavern and authored a bicentennial history of the structure. His knowledge of Charlton history is wide ranging, and the research of its development is a source of great interest to him.

Quentin R. Kuehl was delivered by his grandmother at home and has always called Charlton home. He began school in the one-room schoolhouse near his house and developed a lifelong interest in history. Kuehl spent many hours recording oral histories of old Charltonians who had tales to tell from days gone by. As the years passed, he gained insight into and understanding of the way it was. Most of his working life has been spent on the railroads, another of his great interests. He retired after thirty-seven years of service.

Visit us at
www.historypress.net